FOR ELLE, OUR WARRIOR

YOU ARE NOT ALONE

YES, YOU ARE NOT ALONE!
THE JOURNEY MAY FEEL LONG,
BUT I WANT YOU TO KNOW
YOU HAVE EXACTLY WHAT IT TAKES
BECAUSE YOU BELONG.

Just breathe and remember
that it will get better
and this will be a distant memory
that we both weathered

The sound of my voice is love even when the tears that fall from my face.

And I have to remind myself it takes time to heal and we are working at the speed of your pace.

You are Not Alone

Oh, hey yes you! You are not alone!
I know the beeping of machines may be scary
but trust that God did not bring you
this far so don't grow weary.

Every day and night I will be by your side praying and speaking positive words over you and I know our words will not hide.

A miracle will happen as I trust
the Creator who made you because you are
God's promise straight down from heaven
and we could not wish for anything greater.

THE DAYS ARE COMING OF MILESTONES YOU WILL HIT

YOU ARE NOT ALONE

OH HEY YOU, YES YOU ARE NOT ALONE!
I SEE YOU ARE A WARRIOR AS
YOU KICK YOUR LEGS AND BALL YOUR FIST
YOU MY LOVE WILL QUICKLY GET
THROUGH THE MILESTONE CHECKLIST

YOU WILL BE IN MY ARMS AND OUR
SNUGGLE TIME WILL BE THE MEDICINE
YOU NEED TO GET BETTER.

I CAN'T WAIT TO HOLD YOU SO
WE CAN ALWAYS BE TOGETHER.

EVERY TUBE WILL BE REMOVED
AND THE NEEDLES WILL DISAPPEAR.

YOU MY DEAR WILL SOON YOU WILL BE
IN THE STEPDOWN ROOM AND WE WILL BE
GONE FROM HERE.

Eating from bottles and taking poops will soon be the norm.

But while we wait this journey is teaching me how to love, nurture and stand in the storm.

YOU ARE NOT ALONE

OH HEY YOU, YES YOU ARE NOT ALONE!

YOU ARE A WARRIOR AND

MADE TO BE HERE TO CREATE,

TO DO AND MAKE TREMENDOUS IMPACT

YOUR SOUL SHINES THROUGH AND

THERE IS NOTHING THAT YOU WILL EVER LACK.

YOU ARE NOT ALONE

Marty McDonald
& Baby Elle

CPSIA information can be obtained
at www.ICGtesting.com
Printed in the USA
BVRC100636170821
614313BV00001BA/5